# Grandma Gatewood

## Trail Tales:
## Appalachian
## Trail

**Katherine Seeds Nash**
**Illustrated by Ginger Nielson**

Illustrated by Ginger Nielson

Printed in the United States of America
Published by Braughler Books LLC., Springboro, Ohio

First printing, 2018

ISBN: 978-0-9822187-0-9 softcover
ISBN: 978-0-9822187-9-2 ebook

Library of Congress Control Number: 2018958243

Ordering information: Special discounts are available on quantity purchases by bookstores, corporations, associations, and others. For details, contact the publisher at:

   sales@braughlerbooks.com
   or at 937-58-BOOKS

For questions or comments about this book, please write to:

   info@braughlerbooks.com

**Braughler**™
**Books**
braughlerbooks.com

I dedicate this book to my mother,
Lucy Eleanor Gatewood Seeds,
who dedicated much of her time
preserving and promoting
her mother's legacy.

# Foreword

In 1955, at the age of 67, Grandma Emma Caldwell Gatewood hiked the entire Appalachian Trail, by herself, thus making history as the first woman to do so. She made the journey with very few supplies, including a homemade duffle bag stuffed with a shower curtain, blanket, change of clothing, raisins, saltines, tins of sardines, matches, and journal writing materials. Her minimalistic style is credited for giving rise to the hikers' "ultralite" movement.

Grandma Gatewood's last residence was in Thurman, Ohio, just north of the Ohio River and Gallipolis, where many of the Gatewood relatives lived. While a family reunion was held there, every summer after school was out, most of Katherine's experiences with her were hiking, as her mother and grandmother loved to hike together. Katherine was the youngest grandchild and younger than many of the great-grandchildren, because her mother, Lucy, was Grandma Gatewood's youngest child, the last of eleven.

# CHAPTER ONE

# Grandma's House

"Here we are at Grandma Gatewood's!" Katherine's mom, Lucy, announced.

"Is anyone else going to be here, Mom?" Katherine asked, hopefully. She knew some of her cousins lived nearby. At age seven, Katherine was not interested in adult chitty chat.

"No, Katherine," Mom responded, as she parked the car. "I'm afraid there will be no one for you to play with, today." Katherine frowned, anticipating a lonely day. She remembered Grandma had no TV or toys. Visiting Grandma could be really boring.

Mom pushed open the screen door to the kitchen, letting Katherine in. "Mama!" Lucy called, "We're here!"

Grandma came down the creaky stairs and into the kitchen. Delighted to see them, she gave big hugs to each.

"Ohhhh, I'm so glad you're finally here! I've been itchin' to go for a walk and get some fresh air and sunshine. What say we go see what's kickin' in the crick, out back. Nature is always entertaining!" she quipped.

"Yay!" Katherine exclaimed, beaming with anticipation.

"Mama," Lucy said, as they walked down the road, to the bank of the creek, "Why don't you tell Katherine some stories, from your Appalachian Trail hike?"

"Oooh, I've got plenty of those! That was a long hike!" Grandma Gatewood exclaimed. "I walked clear from Mt. Ogelthorpe, Georgia to Mt. Katahdin, Maine! I started in the Spring and finished in the Fall."

"You hiked ALL Summer?!" Katherine asked, stunned. That's a really long time! You must have stayed in a lot of hotels."

"Oooh, I only stayed at a couple of hotels and a few homes, along the way. Most times I slept under the stars, on a pile of leaves or in a leanto. I didn't even take a tent, because it was too heavy for a 67 year old woman!" Grandma recalled, "Boots are heavy too, so I just wore sneakers."

"What did you do when it rained, Grandma?" Katherine wondered.

"Well, I took an old shower curtain to protect me from the rain. I still got wet as sop, though. I well remember trudging along in wet clothes and then building a fire to dry them off. The fire would warm me up, a bit, too." Grandma reminisced.

"Sometimes rain was the only shower I got," Grandma continued. "From time to time, I'd find a stream in which I could wash my clothes and bathe, but most of the time I was filthy. More than once hotel managers wanted to turn me away, thinking I was a vagrant. That's how much a mess I was!" she chuckled.

# CHAPTER TWO

# Vultures

"Grandma?" Katherine wondered, "When you built a fire, did it keep you safe, from the animals?"

"Oooh, shoot!" Grandma exclaimed, "Most times, I s'pose. But when I was climbing Standing Indian Mountain, in North Carolina, I was tired and the sun was hot, so I didn't build a fire. I just lay down and went to sleep in the leaves."

"I woke up in a little while, feeling like Rip Van Winkle! When I opened my eyes, I saw I was surrounded by a committee of vultures! I yelled at them, shooing them away and shouted 'I ain't dead, yet!'"

They all laughed, visualizing the vultures ready to peck at Grandma!

"That's a funny name, for a flock of vultures, Mama," Lucy remarked.

"You think that's funny, a flock of crows is called a murder!" Grandma laughed. Katherine's eyes popped!

"Not every group of animals is called a flock or herd." Grandma explained, "Groups of vultures actually have different names, depending on what they're doing. If they're pecking at a carcass, they're called a wake of vultures."

"What's a carcass, Grandma?" Katherine asked inquisitively.

Grandma chortled, "A carcass is what the vultures thought I was, Katherine! A carcass is a dead animal and its flesh is called carrion. When something is dead for a while, it starts to decompose and rot. Vultures have a great sense of smell and are able to find it, hidden in the forest, to make a meal of it."

"Oh!" Katherine grimaced, holding her nose, "So you must have smelled really BAD!" They all laughed!

"Don't the vultures get sick eating rotten meat, Grandma?"

"No, Katherine," Grandma continued, "Vultures evolved to clean things up in nature. Dead animals can fester and spread disease. Fun fact about vultures, if you try to catch one, you'll be sorry! To scare you away, they throw up their meal of rotting flesh!"

"Ewwwwwww!!" Mom and Katherine grimaced.

# CHAPTER THREE

# Helping Hand

"Grandma, can we go down the bank, so I can look for salamanders?" Katherine begged.

"Katherine," Mom warned, "I'm not sure Grandma is up to that today."

"Oooh, don't be silly!" Grandma scolded, "I ain't no panytwaist! I may be gettin' older, but I can still get around! This is nothing compared to the challenges on the Appalachian Trail. Why, once on Baldpate Mountain, I had to take a running leap to jump across a crevice! Hiking isn't just a walk in the woods. You have to know and respect nature and how it works."

At the edge of the water, Katherine took off her shoes and stepped into the creek. The cool water and smooth stones were a welcomed sensation, as she gingerly picked up rocks, looking for salamanders. As Katherine went farther into the creek, Mom called, "Watch out for deep water, Katherine!"

Grandma exclaimed, "Oooh, that reminds me of the time I was in the Green Mountains, just past Griffith Lake. I needed to cross a large creek, so swollen from the rain I couldn't find a place safe enough to cross. I sat for quite a spell trying to figure what to do. Luckily two fellers, also hiking the Trail, appeared and we all crossed together. I was secured with rope between the two! The water was so swift, there was a time or two my feet didn't even touch bottom!" she chuckled. "But we made it across…barely! I was so grateful!"

"Most times, if someone offered me help, I was able to help them in return." Grandma reflected. "That evening, when I was ready to bed down, I found the cabin that was meant for hikers. I left it for the boys, returning the favor. The next day I had another opportunity, when I stopped to spend the night, at Grifford Woods Park, at the base of Pico Peak in Vermont. Wouldn't you know those same boys came into the clearing and I was able to share some of the tasty vittles the park official had kindly given me."

"I figured the boys would like some fresh eats. Heaven knows I needed a break from raisins and tins of sardines!" Grandma exclaimed, "Besides, I'm used to working hard and being neighborly. You remember what life was like on the farm, Lucy. It was more work than play!"

"Yes, I remember at just six years old dusting the melons in the field, with lime to keep the bugs off." Mom recalled.

"Hard work and being neighborly is food for the soul!" Grandma quipped.

# CHAPTER FOUR

# Ouch!

"Well," concluded Mom, "We've walked quite a ways and we'll have the same distance on the return, so why don't we head back to the house?"

The three generations of girls climbed back up to the road, pushing brush out of the way as they went.

At the top of the bank, Katherine howled, "Owwww! My arm is burning!" Grandma and Mom rushed over to inspect." Did you brush up against anything, Katherine?" Mom asked.

"Look over there, Lucy!" Grandma directed. "I see a Stinging Nettle bush. Katherine must have brushed up against one. Oooh, when I was on the Trail, just before Damascus, Virginia, I went through the thickest patch of briars and nettles. I was such a mess, I went into town to clean up and treated myself to steak dinner! I know just how Katherine is hurting, right now. Nature's remedy is Jewel Weed and I see some blooming, with orange flowers, over there."

Katherine ran over to the Jewel Weed. She moaned, anxiously, "What do I do with it, Grandma? This really hurts."

"Pull off some leaves, Katherine," Grandma instructed, "crush them and then rub the sap on your arm. That should take the sting away, a bit, until we can get you home and washed up." Katherine did as she was told and agreed, "It does feel a little better, Grandma!"

# CHAPTER FIVE

# Metamorphosis

Now distracted by a butterfly fluttering in the breeze, Katherine skipped ahead. "Grandma, what kind of butterfly is this?"

"I don't know, but I remember seeing one of those, on the Trail in Gold Bond, Virginia."

"That's a Giant Swallowtail," Mom piped in, demonstrating her love of nature she learned from her mom (Grandma). "It looks so bold and beautiful, it must have just emerged from its chrysalis."

Katherine looked at her mother, confused.

Mom explained, "A chrysalis is part of a butterfly's metamorphosis, Katherine. Its life cycle starts as an egg. Then a caterpillar hatches and gorges on leaves, until it is big and plump and ready to become a butterfly. Then it sheds its skin and a hardened shell forms, the chrysalis. The amazing part is, inside, the cells rearrange to make a butterfly! When everything is in place, the adult butterfly splits the shell and emerges!"

"Wow!" Katherine exclaimed, fascinated. "Grandma, what's a flock of butterflies called?"

"I'm so glad you asked, Katherine," Grandma replied, with a big grin. "It is called a kaleidoscope of butterflies!"

Katherine gasped, "That's so beautiful!" Agreeing, Mom nodded her head, emphatically.

"Metamorphosis is such a curious, natural wonder," Grandma mused. "I think that kind of happened to me, on the hike. When I reached the end, I felt like a new person and as free as a butterfly! I was so happy and the view, from Mt. Katahdin, was so stunning I sang 'America the Beautiful' on the spot."

"I knew what an accomplishment it was, as the first woman to hike the entire trail, alone," Grandma remarked, "because there was a crowd of reporters, at the foot of the mountain, waiting for me. I think reporters can go through a metamorphosis when they smell a story and become like a committee of vultures!" They all laughed at the thought of reporters pecking at Grandma, wanting a piece of her so they could tell her story.

When they got back to the house and Katherine got her arm taken care of, Mom announced it was time to head back home, to Gahanna. "This was quite a visit, Mama," she said, kissing her mother's cheek goodbye, "You kept Katherine very entertained!"

Grandma gave Mom and Katherine hugs and bade them farewell. "Until next time! I've got many more stories to share, Katherine!"

APPALACHIAN
TRAIL
2000 miles

KATAHDIN

MAINE

VT.

N.H.

MASS.
R.I.
CONN.

NEW YORK

N.J.

PENNSYLVANIA

DEL.

OHIO    WEST
        VIRGINIA

MD.

VIRGINIA

KY.

NORTH CAROLINA

TENN.

SOUTH
CAROLINA

GEORGIA

SPRINGER

SARDINES

SEEDLESS
RAISINS

# About the Author

Katherine Seeds Nash is Emma Gatewood's youngest grandchild. Katherine had many fun, learning experiences with her mother and Grandma Gatewood on the Appalachian Trail, the Buckeye Trail, and the Seeds family cabin in the Hocking Hills of Ohio. Katherine's love of nature was thus nurtured and led her to a Bachelors in Forest Resources and Conservation, from the University of Florida, and a Masters in Early Childhood Education, from NOVA Southeastern University.

Look for future Grandma Gatewood Trail Tales relaying more stories from the trails and Katherine's childhood memories, on GrandmaGatewoodTrailTales.WordPress.com.

CPSIA information can be obtained
at www.ICGtesting.com
Printed in the USA
BVHW021114250822
645500BV00018B/369